KAMA SUTRA FOR LIFE

KAMA SUTRA FOR LIFE

SOPHIA MORTENSEN

Illustrations by pinglet@pvuk.com

RYLAND
PETERS
& SMALL

LONDON NEW YORK

Senior Designer **Paul Tilby**

Editor **Miriam Hyslop**

Production Manager **Patricia Harrington**

Art Director **Gabriella Le Grazie**

Publishing Director **Alison Starling**

Illustrations **pinglet@pvuk.com**

First published in the
United Kingdom in 2004
by Ryland Peters & Small
20–21 Jockey's Fields
London WC1R 4BW
www.rylandpeters.com

10 9 8 7 6 5 4 3 2

Text, design and illustrations
© Ryland Peters & Small 2004

ISBN-10: 1-84172-724-5
ISBN-13: 978-1-84172-724-0

A CIP record for this book is available
from the British Library.

Printed in China

CONTENTS

INTRODUCTION

You may not know it yet, but you have taken the first steps towards becoming a sensual expert and a divine being! In the West we have a long tradition of being embarrassed about sex, and viewing anything erotic as sinful or dirty. In the East, particularly in India, China and Japan, sexual exploration has long been regarded as one of the most effective ways to achieve spiritual enlightenment. If you haven't previously thought about sex as a sacred act, then *Kama Sutra for Life* may change your mind. Kama Sutra isn't only about lovemaking positions — by learning a little about the philosophy behind the Tantric teachings and practising some simple techniques, you will begin to feel more creative and focused in other areas of your life, too. Alongside the undoubted benefits of enjoying mind-blowing sex, you will also feel more healthy, energized and optimistic — and, let's face it, we can all use a little more energy and optimism to get us through our busy lives.

It is easy to think that the Kama Sutra has no place in the modern Western bedroom, being impractical and requiring far too much effort and time. This is not the case. A few simple changes in lifestyle can really make a positive difference to your spiritual and sexual wellbeing and help create harmony in your home and in your relationships. It really works! You don't have to contort yourself into unnatural positions to start practising. Maybe Kama Sutra is something you have wanted to learn about for some time but you had not found the right book. Maybe it is something totally new to you. Either way, it doesn't matter how much or how little you know about it; if you are looking for a way to introduce more passion and sensuality into your relationship and your life, then this is the perfect place to start. *Kama Sutra for Life* will provide you with lots of ideas and exercises that will transform your love life and bring you and your partner more pleasure than you would have thought possible.

The Tantric teachings speak a lot about energy – the essential life force that flows through all living things, and which needs to keep moving in order to keep us operating effectively and healthily. When we get stuck in a sexual routine that follows a predictable pattern, we run the risk of getting stale, and our relationships can lose that essential spark of magic. Practising the Kama Sutra can help to keep our sexual energies charged with love and joy. Once we open ourselves up to our partners and begin to examine our sensual selves, we are on the path to ultimate pleasure, bringing the exotic, the divine and the exquisite into our lives. You can start a life of harmonious loving right now! Don't let your sex life follow the same routine. The next time you and your partner are in the mood, consciously do something different and get those energies flowing. Once you have digested this book, you will have learned a new lexicon of love. You will become familiar with how perfumes function on our erotic senses, how correct breathing can prolong orgasm, and how to adapt your lovemaking to your natural rhythms. Even if some of the terminology and ideas seem a little unusual, *Kama Sutra for Life* will explain everything clearly and practically. Once you enter the Tantric realm, a new world of sensuality will open up to you – a treasure store of delights that will revolutionise your love life. So, enter a world where gods and goddesses make love with each other in a perfumed paradise; where the entire world around you will take on an erotic flavour and stimulate you – body, mind and spirit. Enter the exotic world of Tantric love and total sensuality. *Om Shanti!*

PART ONE

THE TEMPLE OF THE BODY

ORIGINS OF THE KAMA SUTRA

The original Kama Sutra originated in India in the second century A.D. Created in Sanskrit, the world's oldest form of writing, by a sage named Vatsyayana, it is the earliest of numerous Hindu love manuals. Early British explorers in India were shocked by the voluptuous statues they encountered on their travels, and astonished by the level of sophistication that was regarded as normal sexual practice. It was Sir Richard Burton, the eminent Victorian explorer with a taste for the exotic, who, in 1883, translated the Kama Sutra into the Queen's English and brought it to Britain. Quite what the Queen thought of it one can only guess, but its secrets were only made widely available when the censorship laws relaxed in the 1960s. The ancient love texts were not written to excite their audience in the way that authors in the West produced erotic books as aids to masturbation. They were not intended to be lewd or crude; indeed, this 'theology of love' was written with the serious intention of acquainting people, as early as possible, with all the information they needed to give their partner ultimate pleasure.

WHAT IS TANTRA?

Tantra is an all-embracing philosophy of spirituality, science and art that has eroticism at its core. The Tantric approach to life is joyful and sensual, and regards the sexual energies as sacred. The dynamic life force that builds within us from the first stirrings of arousal through to the exquisite explosion of orgasm can be consciously used to improve our overall wellbeing. Western philosophy has a long history of separating the body from the mind. 'I think, therefore I am' said Descartes, one of the founders of modern logical thought. Putting a division between the body and the mind doesn't make sense in Tantric philosophy, in which the main principle is the idea of interconnectedness — the link between ourselves and the universe we inhabit — body, mind *and* spirit. If we divide a person up into parts and do not treat ourselves as an interconnected whole, we can easily get out of balance — a surefire way to illness and depression. By following a more holistic lifestyle, physically, spiritually and sexually, we can become healthier, relaxed, and more pleasant to be around.

FINDING TIME FOR PLEASURE

*T*he Kama Sutra says we should never accept 'mediocre sexual congress', and that applies to both sexes. Women should not just lie back and let the man do all the work! The most common cause for sexual relationships breaking down is not jealousy or being 'no good' in bed; it is because one or both parties in a relationship are regularly too tired for sex. There are so many demands on us in modern life that we can easily find ourselves exhausted and stressed, unable to be at our best in the bedroom. Quality, not quantity, is the key to keeping relationships harmonious. Interpreting the Kama Sutra in a modern context, sharing 'quality time' with our partners is extremely important to keeping our energies flowing and our batteries charged. Set aside one evening a week where you can be together, undisturbed, and where the TV will not be switched on. This night is for you and your darling to give and receive pleasure — to play and be joyful in each other's company and know the exquisite delights of mutual satisfaction. Read the 'Kama Sutra at Home' section (pages 22–37) to obtain some ideas for a night of sizzling passion that will make you feel great.

THE LEXICON OF LOVE

LINGAM AND YONI

In the West, the words we use to name our sexual parts are either crude or funny. We have disassociated our bodies from a sense of the sacred, and we do not always treat them with the respect they deserve, eating junk food and drinking too much alcohol. In the East, the body is a sacred temple and it is taught that we should worship all of it, including the genitals — the lingam (phallus) and yoni (vagina). The penis is given affectionate terms in the East including: ambassador, general, hero, flute, jade sceptre, jade stalk, monk and tiger. The lingam is thought to have an extrovert 'personality', being outside the body and often in a good mood! The yoni is more mysterious, seen as the entrance to a sacred shrine and treated with reverence. Names for the yoni include: oyster, honey pot, shady valley, peach, knot, shell, anemone, jade gate, open melon and phoenix. The erect lingam is a direct representation of the god Shiva in all his creative potency and the yoni is the all-powerful image of femininity, a manifestation of the awesome goddess, Kali. When we unite the lingam with the yoni, ecstatic energies build up as we 'worship' at the altar.

BHAKTI AND SHAKTI

When embarking on the journey of love we need to put our trust in another person. This requires Bhakti – faith or devotion. The second element in this sacred pairing of emotions is Shakti, the creative energy that resides in human sexuality and which is evoked during love-making. When we recognize the Shakti element within our partner, we should respond with Bhakti, forming the loving union that flows between two people when they're about to share their sexual energies. The god Shiva is the male aspect of Shakti. He is the immortal divine principle, the Lord of all things. His symbol is the erect lingam – a great cosmic erection! Hindu mythology teaches that the entire universe is born out of the joining of Shiva with Shakti, and the love-play of these divine entities causes the moon to wax and wane. Your own sexual congress may not cause the heavens to move, but you will feel the sacred love energy flowing between you and replenishing your devotion to each other.

KUNDALINI 'SERPENT' POWER

Kundalini is the deep-seated creative/sexual energy that smoulders within us all. Esoteric teachings speak of the kundalini energy as a coiled snake, slow to unwind but all-powerful once roused. It is said that one can direct the kundalini energy out through the eyes and into those of another person, entrancing them sexually. Sexual contact and certain forms of yoga can uncoil the kundalini Shakti – which resides at the base of the spine, near to the sexual centre. One way to raise the kundalini is to practise 'breath of fire'. Sit quietly by yourself, preferably cross-legged on the floor. Inhale deeply through the nostrils and expand your diaphragm, then exhale through your nostrils, pressing the stomach back towards the spine. After a few breaths, increase the pace, co-ordinating your belly movements with the breath in rapid succession so that your out-breath – always through the nostrils – sounds like a steam train. After a minute of 'breath of fire' clench your anal muscles and sexual organs, pulling the energy up through your body and visualizing it as a molten gold liquid coursing through you, giving you a dynamic infusion of power.

THE CHAKRAS

*I*nside each of us is a network of nerves and sensory organs that interprets the physical world. Tantra teaches us we also have several invisible centers of energy — the chakras, meaning 'wheels' in Sanskrit — that determine our physical, intellectual, emotional and spiritual well-being, and which we can activate or close down at will. According to Vedic tradition, the chakras are located along the central meridian of the body and are the seat of major vortexes of emotion. The seven centres are numbered from one — the root or *muladhara* chakra, located in the genital area — up to seven, at the crown of the head. In between are chakras located at the navel, spleen, heart, throat, and between the eyes — the *anja* (or 'third eye') chakra. Each chakra is associated with a colour of the spectrum. The two important chakras in Kama Sutra are, unsurprisingly, the *muladhara* and *sacral* (navel) chakras. To be receptive to the sexual energies, spend a few moments each week using 'breath of fire' technique — as described on p. 16 — to breathe kundalini energy into these areas. Direct your energy to your *muladhara* chakra, visualizing the colour red. Then breathe into your *sacral* chakra, visualizing the colour orange, which controls creativity. Regular balancing of your chakras in this way will help to keep your sexual energies flowing.

THE 64 ARTS

The Kama Sutra promotes self-improvement and self-expression in all the Arts, and recommends that the art of lovemaking should be perfected. The art of love was given place of honour in ancient Hindu philosophy, but it was intimately associated with the other '64 Arts', including singing, dancing, painting, flower-arranging, sewing, reading, drawing, charm-making, sports, carpentry, cooking, perfumery, language, etiquette and the art of disguise! The Hindu texts teach us that the Arts are likened to the flames of an inner sun – located in our solar plexus (or *sacral* chakra) – that radiates within us. Even the Western name for this part of the body has a reference to the original Hindu word meaning 'sun'. The flames should purify us, burn up all negativity, and bring about creative transformation – making our bodies and minds ready to enjoy total pleasure. In the next section, you will find out how to put more art into your lovemaking. Now you have learned to build your sexual energies, it's time to set the scene for seduction, Kama Sutra style.

PART TWO

KAMA SUTRA AT HOME

THE PLEASURES OF LIFE

*D*on't rush anything when you practise Kama Sutra. Learn to be
a sensualist. Our sense of the erotic is evoked through the exquisite
contact of our senses with the external world. All the pleasures of life –
eating, drinking, grooming and lovemaking – should be approached as
if they were a fine art. Imagine you are a princess (or prince) in your own
home. Treat every meal, however simple, as a banquet to be savoured; every
bath or shower a luxurious cascade of cleansing liquid. Take time to reward
yourself. The technique of creative visualization is very popular in Eastern
mysticism. So, before you create a temple out of your body and the place
where you are going to practise Kama Sutra, take a few moments to
visualize yourself as an alluring, exotic creature – a goddess (or god)
weaving a spell that will hypnotize your partner into a reverie of erotic
delights. Believe it, visualize it, and it shall be so.

AN EROTIC TEMPLE OF YOUR OWN

You can easily turn your living space into a temporary erotic temple and create a feeling of harmony and exoticism. Western architecture is very harsh, with lots of angles and corners, so soften the hard edges with drapes, throws, wall hangings, rugs and cushions — a must for the modern Tantric temple. As far as possible, try to use natural fabrics: silks, handwoven rugs, muslin drapes. Keep the furniture at a low level. If you usually sit upright at a dining table for a candlelight dinner, this time present a variety of delicious food in small bowls and serve low, as you eat sitting on cushions on the floor. Even if you live in a streamlined, modern home, introduce some natural elements into the room. Fresh flowers, plants and floating candles are ideal. Sprinkle the area where you plan to make love with petals and natural perfume. The combination of low lighting, colourful fabrics, incense (oil burners, not sticks), flowers and the right music, will create the perfect atmosphere for a night of seduction. All you need to add is you, looking fabulously exotic.

SEDUCTION TECHNIQUES

You are taking the time to set the scene, to treat yourself and your partner to an evening of exquisite sensual delight. Indulge yourself in the pleasure of seduction. Tantra says that sexual desire goes through four stages: the smile, the gaze, the embrace and full sexual union. We can visualize each of these four 'stages of ecstasy' as the four elements of air, water, earth and fire. Take your time. Try to bring about four different types of consciousness as your seduction progresses through each stage: attraction, eye contact, body contact and actual sex. Once you are at the stage of actual sex, you should free yourself of all inhibitions. The Tantric texts say: 'when filled with sexual desire, you should not know any shame or restraint with your partner'. If you consciously spend time relishing each stage of the seduction process, you will build your arousal and energy levels to an exquisite crescendo. By the time you are ready for full sexual union with your partner your desire will be 'fuelled' to the extent that your orgasms will be much more powerful.

BATHING

Water is a sacred element, covering much of our planet. Being close to water relaxes or invigorates us. Think of the different feelings we experience when we are beside the crashing waves of the ocean, a calm lake or tinkling fountain. Waterfalls or cold showers produce health-giving negative ions, which have a stimulating effect on our well-being. The yogic texts tell us we should never bring the day's residues into the bedroom, therefore we need to wash the office, the kitchen and the outdoor world from our bodies and psyches before we make love. When we bathe or shower we are purifying ourselves from the many pollutants we have to encounter in our daily lives, particularly in towns, cities, roads and on transport systems. Whenever you have the opportunity, try to bathe and make love outdoors – in the sea, in waterfalls, in rivers or streams. Many religions advocate washing only in running water. In the West we are very fond of the 'nice hot bath', which is warming and relaxing, but we should take care to avoid lying in our own grime! If a bath is too hot, it can make us drowsy, so it is best to bathe in this way only before sleeping. Cold water splashed on the back of the neck or a quick blast with a cold shower after a hot bath is excellent for the circulation.

PERFUME

*P*erfume works on a subtle but deep level, stimulating our desires and supersensory faculties. It is thought that a person's natural scent can determine whether or not we are attracted to them. This olfactory means of communication is unconscious. In olden times, courtesans were known to dab their own sexual secretions behind their ears! Don't spray yourself with chemical concoctions – these deaden your natural scent. Instead, use natural oils and essences, which are known to energize and uplift the spirit. This is why they are used in religious rites. At the very least they help to create a harmonious atmosphere and provoke contentment. Synthetic perfumes may be attractively packaged but they tend to be too strong for Kama Sutra – which incorporates the sweeter, more subtle aromas of sandalwood, lemon, myrrh, jasmine, patchouli, saffron and basil. It is easy to find essential oils in natural health stores. Even your high street chemist stocks a good range of aromatherapy products. To fill your boudoir with exotic fragrance, add some essential oils to a little water in a plant sprayer and squirt!

ADORNMENT

dornment of the female form transforms a woman into a living goddess! From ancient times people have enhanced the raw material of their bodies. Our earliest ancestors painted directly onto their skin and made necklaces and earrings out of bone, feathers and clay beads. It was in ancient Egypt and Babylonia, however, when adornment evolved into a more sophisticated art. Make-up, jewellery and headdresses were status symbols used to indicate rank and privilege. The colour red has always played a leading role in make-up, and is known to stimulate male arousal, subconsciously signifying the inflamed genitals. The many paintings and carvings that illustrate the Kama Sutra feature women decorated with flowers in the hair, bracelets, necklaces, head ornaments, waist and ankle chains and exotic make-up. Forget what's in fashion and experiment with wilder make-up techniques than those you are used to. Use eye-liner and kohl to enhance your eyes and decorate your body with stick-on sparkly jewels. And there is nothing as pretty as delicate fresh flowers woven into the hair for a really feminine touch.

MUSIC & DANCING

*I*t goes without saying that chill-out music is best for an evening of sensuality. Indian classical music is delightful. Lovemaking is better against a backdrop of instrumental music, as lyrics can impinge on your own language of love. With music there is always dancing, one of the 64 Arts. Ancient Indian temples excelled in displays of erotic dance. In some temples, as many as 500 yogically trained *devadasis* would be in attendance, working devotees into a state of heightened arousal, their colourful diaphanous robes twirling around them as they displayed their snake-hipped skills. One Tantric poem declares 'the dancing girl has the power to initiate the process of sexual rejuvenation'. There is no reason why you cannot put on a dancing display for your lover in your own living room! Forget the lewd posturing of the lap-dancer and cultivate a powerful seduction through more subtle, alluring movements and adornments that enhance but do not vulgarize the female form. Undulate your hips and sway your body to instrumental Indian classical music, caressing yourself in long languid strokes. You may like to perform a 'dance of seven veils' using exotic fabrics in ways that tease and tantalize your partner, revealing just enough flesh to be sexy, but always leaving something to the imagination.

KAMA SUTRA IN THE KITCHEN

Many cultures incorporate food into their sacred rituals. In Tantra, all food is thought of as nourishing the spirit as well as the body, so it is important to choose wisely what you serve to your lover. Eating is the next most sensual thing to making love. When cooking for a sexually charged night in, unplug that microwave, because you are going to be using fresh ingredients. Also, try to use foods that are in season. It is most fitting, of course, when having a Kama Sutra night in, to cook dishes from an Indian recipe. Small bowls of spiced lentils, vegetable curries and yoghurt served with basmati rice and chutneys are ideal. Don't over-season your food; practise skill and modesty with spices. Try cardamom, cumin, fenugreek and garam masala rather than generic supermarket 'curry powder'. Remember that vegetables are easily and quickly digested, and provide a fast-track energy source that will not give you the uncomfortably full sensation of meat — which is not recommended for a passionate night in as it takes too long to digest. For dessert, fresh succulent fruit and a natural or quality ice-cream makes for an indulgent counterbalance to a spicy main course. Mangoes, strawberries, peaches and stewed plums are all very good with ice-cream. The golden rule is moderation. You should finish your meal wanting just a little more.

APHRODISIACS

The best aphrodisiac is a healthy lifestyle! Regular fresh air, exercise and fresh foods will ensure you maintain your sexual energy at optimum levels. Balance and harmony are the key words in Kama Sutra living. Tantric practitioners recommend the following as having aphrodisiac qualities, but little and often is always going to produce the best results and, of course, these should be taken in moderation: asparagus, fennel, figs, almonds, raisins, pomegranates, walnuts, red onions, cinnamon, fenugreek, celery, nutmeg, ginger root, ginseng root and licorice. It is also known that fresh parsley, thyme and lettuce aid sexual appetite. The *Kama Sutra for Life* would not be complete without a few naughty western indulgences, though. Alcohol in moderation is fine for loosening inhibitions and getting in the mood, but that means a couple of glasses of good wine or naturally brewed beer rather than several cans of lager! Also, for a really sensuous treat, try strawberries dipped in melted organic chocolate. Chocolate contains trace minerals that are said to enhance the libido and have the same effect on the brain as falling in love. The combination of the tang of fresh fruit and melted sweetness is perfect for a double dose of oral satisfaction.

EROTIC MASSAGE

$\mathcal{M}$assage is one of the most effective ways we can connect with a partner on a deeper, more sensual level. It should be a reciprocal undertaking and, thinking always of balance and harmony, be sure that both 'sides' of a person get equal treatment. For instance, never massage only one foot, or one hand. The person giving the massage should be calm and meditative on their partner's wellbeing, and intuitive to their needs. The masseur should draw up loving, healing or sexual energy from their *whole body* and transfer it to the person being massaged — visualizing a different colour energy flowing out of the hands for the particular mood you wish to create or which chakra you are nearest to. The person giving the massage should come out of the experience almost as relaxed and energized as the person being massaged. Make sure the room is warm and that the oil you are using is heated to at least body temperature. There are plenty of sensual oils available but look out for erotic fragrances such as sandalwood, ylang ylang, orange neroli, tangerine, frankincense, ginger, geranium, patchouli, rose, cedarwood, tangerine and vetiver.

When massaging the body, have your partner lying comfortably, face down. One way of alluding to the sensual nature of the massage is to press your palm on his sacrum – the small of his back, just above his tail bone – and gently rock him from side to side, opening him up to receiving your sensual healing touch. This is both reassuring and arousing, working on the first three chakras, which deal with sexuality, creativity and security. When massaging the back use a graceful but firm flowing action and keep to the flesh of the back, avoiding the actual spine but sliding your bunched fists or thumbs upwards alongside it. Always work upwards, building your partner's *chi* towards the top of the head. Be intuitive – there is no hard and fast rule that dictates where on the body you should begin and end, although starting with the feet and ending with the head is usual. On the calves and shoulders, use the pads of your thumbs, pushing upwards in small circular movements. Avoid actual genital contact; by concentrating your thoughts and energies on sensuality, your partner will be suitably aroused by the time you have finished. Don't actually massage your partner's penis with oil as this can be an irritant for some people. Instead, an oral massage will always be welcome!

PART THREE

THE FIRES OF LOVE

TYPES OF WOMAN & MAN

Much of the Kama Sutra uses the natural world as a reference point for its sexual terminology. Our ancestors lived in close proximity to the natural world, and took their influences from an environment abundant with flowers, animals, shells and flowers. Eastern sexual philosophy seeks harmony and balance in all unions. The ancient Indian love texts categorize men and women into three different types according to the dimensions of their genitals. It is recommended that the types match each other as closely as possible, although specific lovemaking postures allow for 'unequal' pairings and each type has its own desirable quality.

TYPES OF WOMAN

The deer Her yoni is no longer than five inches in depth. She has an active mind, eats moderately and is well proportioned with good breasts. She has a soft, tender body and delights in the pleasures of lovemaking. Her yoni has the perfume of the lotus flower.

The mare Her yoni is no longer than seven inches in depth. She is adaptable and even of temperament, being affectionate and graceful. She likes a high standard of living and lots of relaxation. Her body is delicate and she has beautiful eyes. She is slow to come to her climax.

The elephant Her yoni is about ten inches in depth. She has large breasts, a wide face and somewhat short limbs. She enjoys the pleasures of life and has a tendency to over-indulgence. Her love juice is abundant.

TYPES OF MAN

The hare His lingam is approximately five inches when erect. He is usually short of stature but well proportioned and with an even disposition. His emissions are sweet.

The bull His lingam is about seven inches when erect. This is a robust man who is always keen to make love. He often has a high forehead and large eyes and is of an active disposition.

The horse His lingam is around nine to ten inches long and belongs to a type that is tall, big-boned and with a deep voice. He can be possessive and gluttonous, although passionate. His semen is copious and often salty.

COMPATIBILITY

According to Kama Sutra, it is ideal if 'equal' sexual pairings are made: the deer with the hare; the mare with the bull and the elephant with the horse. It says: 'when the proportions of both lovers are alike, then satisfaction is easy to achieve. The greatest happiness consists in the correspondence of dimensions.' In the West, we should interpret this perhaps less literally, where we are also told that 'opposites attract'. Often we find that very different personalities, if not body types, complement each other in a relationship. For instance, it's good if one partner excels in organizational skills or has a good sense of direction — spiritually and practically. If a couple is too alike, there can be a locking of horns, to continue the animal theme. If neither has much practical sense, a relationship can drift into vagueness and not charge itself with enough dynamic energy. *Kama Sutra for Life* would say that any couple, whatever their body shape and size, can have a harmonious sexual relationship if there is giving and receiving on both sides.

It is important for the Kama Sutra couple to show interest in each other's occupations and hobbies, complementing each other's interests and talents with variety and fresh energy. Over-familiarity can sometimes breed animosity, whether it's the places you visit together or if you are spending too much 'dead' time together, i.e. watching TV. It is beneficial for a couple to spend time apart, reflecting on their own and their partner's personality and unique essence, thinking of ways to honour and worship that person with special treats and little tokens of love and affection. Never take your partner for granted. The Tantra teaches us that 'like begets like'. Approach your partner with an open heart and a generous spirit, and you will be rewarded by the same feelings. Particularly remember not to bring the day's residues into the sacred space of your union. Don't pour out the pent-up stresses of the working day onto your partner; this may set the tone for the whole evening. Instead, try to download your stresses beforehand, or set aside time to talk through each other's hassles out of the sexual zone.

LOVE POSITIONS LYING DOWN

Mare's Position The woman lies down with her legs together and tightly squeezes her partner's lingam inside her yoni. Her legs are inside his, and this causes a delicious friction for both lovers. This position is particularly useful for the mare and elephant types.

Splitting a Bamboo She lies back against a big cushion, and he enters her. She then places one of her legs on her partner's shoulder and stretches the other leg out along the bed. After a few moments she reverses the procedure so the other leg is on his shoulder and her opposite leg stretched out. This position is perfect for equally matched types.

Packed Position The woman lies down flat, raises her thighs bent at the knee and crosses one leg over the other. He then enters her. This position creates a very snug fit between the lingam and yoni and is good for hare/bull men when with mare/elephant women, or when his lingam is smaller than her yoni.

Yawning Position She lies back, raises her thighs and keeps them wide apart held at the knee during lovemaking. Good for bull and horse men or when accommodating a lover with a large lingam.

LOVE POSITIONS LYING DOWN

Opening and Blossoming She lies on her back and lifts both legs straight up, feet pointing to the ceiling. He inserts his lingam into her, taking hold of her legs and bringing them together. Their thighs should be pressed very closely together.

The Crab The man and woman both lie on their sides. He lies between her thighs with one of her legs under him and one thrown over him so that she can pull him into her.

Wheel of Kama The man sits between the legs of the woman, who is lying on her back. He holds her legs wide apart, and he stretches his arms as far as he possibly can on both sides of her. He should move her body around underneath him.

The Bow She lies back with cushions under her hips to raise her sexual parts. Her back should be arched like a bow. Then the man aims his lingam into her like the arrow. A very popular position good for all types.

LOVE POSITIONS ACTIVE

Position of a Cow A rear-entry position. She is on all fours but with her feet on the floor rather than her knees. She bends forward with her hands resting on a low table. Her lover enters her and pays as much attention to her back as he would to her breasts if they were facing.

Pair of Tongs The woman sits on top of the man with her knees drawn up and her feet placed either side of his hips. She eases herself onto his erect lingam and holds it in her by pressing her thighs together. In this position lovemaking can last a long time as deep thrusting is not easily achieved.

Self-created Position The man sits with his legs crossed and the woman is on his lap with knees bent and either side of him. She should slightly raise one leg by putting a hand under her foot. By moving her leg around, she can create exquisite sensations.

LOVE POSITIONS ACTIVE

Suspended Position The man supports himself against a wall or tree and the woman sits on his joined-together hands with her legs wrapped around his waist, her arms thrown around his neck, and her feet pressing into whatever the man is leaning against. This is ideal for a very strong man and a light woman. For those who find this difficult, a modern interpretation would have the woman sitting on the edge of a table.

The Swing The woman sits on top of the man, who raises his middle so that he can flex himself up and down in a reverse of a push-up. For a variation the woman faces away from him so he has the glorious sight of her buttocks moving up and down.

Turning Position From making love face-to-face, the man turns the woman under him without removing his lingam from her yoni, enjoying the feeling of their tangled limbs chafing each other.

SENSUAL MASTER CLASS

TAKING KAMA SUTRA FURTHER

Some readers may want to delve deeper into the Tantric mysteries that we only have space to outline here. One of the advanced-level practices is seminal retention — where the man deliberately holds back his orgasm. Known as 'guarding the flame', it is a discipline that is supposed to enhance creativity, productivity and mental alertness and requires amazing powers of resistance. One way of doing this is to bring pressure on the perineum — the zone between the scrotum and the anus — with the middle and forefingers of the left hand. It is also useful to hold off ejaculation through varying the strokes during lovemaking. Try one deep stroke into the yoni for every three short ones; then increase to one for every five, and so on until one for every nine shallow strokes. Another way of taking the Kama Sutra further is for a couple to perform a Tantric love ritual, where you spend a whole day making love, building your kundalini energies together to a point where you will experience an explosion of pleasure so fulfilling that you will never think about sex in the same way again. The ritualized breathing, chanting and honouring of each other enables your egos to dissolve. This is where you can access sexual love energies on a higher spiritual plain, tapping directly into the sacred universal fires as you move towards truly mind-blowing orgasms.

KISSING & TOUCHING

The Kama Sutra regards any physical contact between lovers as a form of embrace, and it even teaches many types of lovers' greeting, each one involving more intimacy.

Twining Creeper The woman should raise one leg and twine it around her man like a tree creeper, pulling him into her body. She kisses him repeatedly, drawing his head to hers in both hands.

Climbing a Tree The woman should place one of her feet on his and raise the other leg to the height of this thigh, passionately pressing herself against him. She then encircles his waist and should hold and press him forcibly as if about to climb up him. She should bend her body over his and kiss him as if she were drinking the elixir of life.

Embrace of the Breasts Man and woman should meet in a way so that both sets of nipples press into each other. He should close his eyes and they should hold the position long enough to create erotic sensations.

Embrace of the Thighs Either the man or woman presses one or both thighs of the other between his or her legs.

Rice and Seed The couple should hold each other closely so that the arms and thighs of one are totally encircled by those of the other. Contact should be made between the lingam and yoni.

SCRATCHING & BITING

*S*cratching and biting, similar to that seen in animal play, is considered to be invigorating during lovemaking and an expression of ecstatic passion for your partner. Teeth and nails can be used to stimulate erogenous zones. Pressing skillfully with the nails into the flesh of the breasts, buttocks, thighs and armpits heightens arousal. Grazing your partner lightly with your nails will cause goosebumps and delicious shivers of pleasure to course through their body. The gentle biting of your partner's neck during love play, especially from behind, such as performed by big cats, is a wonderful display of the enjoyment of the sexual act. The places on the body that can be bitten are the same as those that can be kissed, and the Kama Sutra speaks of a variety biting styles:

Hidden Bite Reddening of the skin that is caused by sucking – the classic 'lovebite'.
Swollen Bite Where pressure is brought from pinching and sucking.
Point Bite Nips from two teeth.
Rosary of Points Small amounts of skin bitten with all teeth.
Coral and Jewels Bringing together teeth and lips.
Broken Cloud Grazing and love bites of the breasts.

ORAL TECHNIQUES

*O*ral-genital sex requires us to become aware of the natural musky aromas of our partner and relish their individual scent.

Lingam-loving Try the 'omen-making' technique – plump up your moistened lips and, with your head at a sideways angle, draw your lips along his lingam without actually taking it inside your mouth. This is a useful alternative for women who gag easily or for those with 'horse' type lovers!

Yoni-honouring The yoni is the original lotus flower, with many folds and 'leaves'. Like a mouth, it has two lips and a tongue – the clitoris, the starburst pearl of a woman's pleasure. The man should approach the yoni as if he were drinking from a life-giving fountain. This is the place to use the tongue to bring her to a state of climax or heightened arousal.

Together What we call '69' in the West is 'the crow' in Tantra. This is the oral position that allows for 'mutual nourishment'. The woman should try to harmonize the movements of her mouth and yoni to the point where her partner loses himself in the all-enveloping essence of the female energies. The close contact of his mouth with her yoni energy is said to stimulate the pineal and pituitary glands to release chemicals that open the third eye. His erect lingam exudes electrical energy that will feed her kundalini, bringing about an exchange of energies that envelop the couple in loving harmony and psychic protection.

KAMA SUTRA FOR ALL SEASONS

Before we lived in houses and surrounded ourselves with the trappings of modern life, we consorted with our partners in the natural world, having close contact with the changing seasons – being aware of the ever-turning wheel of life. The Kama Sutra refers to environments and elements that are unfamiliar to Westerners, such as temples and lotus blossoms, but one way modern couples can reconnect with the universal creative force is to make love outdoors at least once each season. This will be easier in the summer, when you are on holiday, possibly in a hot climate, but try to find the time to go on a country walk in autumn and enjoy the earthy scents of the season as you caress each other in the woods. Make love standing next to a tree in the winter, protected by big coats, woolly scarves and hats as the frosty air swirls around you. Celebrate the dawn of spring by playfully chasing each other across the local park and buying each other flowers. By using your sexual energies to honour the rhythms of the universe you will be tapping into the sacred systems of meaning dictated by nature. And that's auspicious!

ADVANCED POSITIONS

Elephant Position The woman lies down so her breasts, stomach and thighs are all in contact with the bed. The man then comes from behind to extend himself over her body, caressing her sides and feeling the glorious voluptuousness of her curves. He should enter her with his lower back curved in, working his way into her from underneath. Meanwhile, she arches her back inwards to propel her yoni into an accessible position. Although she is facing away from him, her movements should be proudly erotic, lewd and encouraging.

Tantric Tortoise She is underneath him, with her right leg resting on his left shoulder. From this position she should place the soles of both feet into the middle of his chest, imagining herself being created from his heart. He should press her knees with his arms and control his breathing. This position can help the couple realize enlightenment and deep love for each other.

Bee Buzzing Position Also known as the Kali posture, this is a rare 'woman on top' position. She is to coax his semen from him similar to how a bee gets a flower to release its pollen. He lies full length on the ground while she squats over his thighs, closing her legs together once he is deep within her. From here she moves her hips in a circular motion, churning and milking him to climax. She can thoroughly satisfy herself in this position, too.

FORMING A PRIMAL UNION

While much Tantric philosophy is lofty and aspirational, this is complemented by some very earthy advice. One of the ways a couple can bond emotionally is for them not to wash for at least an hour after climaxing. It is important that something of each other's essences soaks into both bodies, forming a 'primal psychic union' between two individuals. Most often this would occur when a couple make love at night, before sleeping, but it is also important that this happens at some point when both stay awake, so each person can learn to recognize the unique scents they form together. We can learn much from the animal kingdom in this respect — it makes sense to think of marking a lover with our scent. In many ways we have aspired to becoming as unlike animals as is possible; in the West we are repulsed by our own bodily functions and dubious of anything that reminds us we are mammals. While adorning ourselves with make-up and perfume and dressing ourselves to be as attractive as possible form a major part of human sexual play, we shouldn't neglect all of our primal passions.

KAMA SUTRA FOREVER

I hope this *Kama Sutra for Life* has given you some ideas for thinking differently about your love life. By treating sex as an act of sacred celebration we can all become experts of pleasure, radiating that positive glow that shines out of people who are in touch with their sensual selves. We all have vast reserves of inner strength and access to the rejuvenating life force that is part of our universe. No matter how sluggish we are feeling we can instantly energize ourselves through tapping into the kundalini energy or by accessing the healing properties of the natural world. Kama Sutra doesn't have to be about perfecting tricky lovemaking positions, although I would recommend yoga to anyone as the form of exercise most beneficial to great sex — and there is no harm in becoming more supple. The modern world is extremely competitive and aggressive, and it is very important to make time for love and to treat ourselves to the things we find aesthetically pleasing. Living a Kama Sutra lifestyle means that we can express our sensual selves in the most delightful ways — giving and receiving the pleasure that will keep our bodies healthy, our minds positive and our spirit joyful. *Om Nama Shivaya*.